SANTA and the Christ Child

A Christmas Classic
by
Nicholas Bakewell
Illustrations by
Herbert Rayburn

This book is based on my copy-righted screenplay entitled
"SANTA AND THE CHRIST CHILD."
May it fill your hearts with love and joy and the real spirit of Christmas!

MERRY CHRISTMAS

Hello from Santa's House!...

This is Santa Claus speaking to tell you about a sequence of amazing and unforgettable events. . . .

It all started while I was feeding the reindeer one morning, just a few weeks before Christmas . . .

. . . I was surprised to find a young boy asleep in the stable,

. . . a handsome child . . . who just begged to stay and see how we prepared for Christmas . . .

I agreed, and took
him around the village
to introduce him to the elves . . .

When we got to the carpenter shop he was
especially attracted to that, and wanted
to know if he could help out there . . .

(. . . It turned out
he had quite an aptitude! . .)

The Child just endeared himself to
everyone — and everything was going just
great. I was especially pleased, as we
were ahead of schedule on the inventory . . .

Then, just when everything was going so well
— tragedy struck! While out searching for a
lost reindeer, I slipped on the ice, fell and
broke my leg . . .

The doctor put on a cast and said, "Well, that's it! . Your trip is off. Christmas is only two weeks away. There is no way you can make the trip this year . . ."

What a disaster! . . .
Everyone was terribly upset
and dejected — except the
Child. He went right on
working in the carpenter
shop making toys. He
moved into my house
so he could kind'a
look after me . . .

He exercised the reindeer everyday . . .

And he made me a
beautiful set of wooden
crutches . . . so I could at
least hobble around a bit . . .

In addition to all of those activities, he was working on a 'secret project' in the carpenter shop. He had it all screened off so no one could see what it was . . . The elves were just about bursting with curiosity — and finally tried to sneak past him to see the 'secret project' . . .

He caught them, though, and said, "If you'll get to work and

finish up these toys —
that would please Santa very much — then
I'll show you the 'secret project' . . ."

The elves agreed and quickly got back
to work. On Christmas eve they finished
up the very last toy — so the Child
pulled aside the screen. You should
have seen the excited
expressions on the
faces of those elves
when they saw the
wonderful . . .
"secret project! . . ."

I was here in the house, of course, with my bad leg and all . . . It was Christmas Eve and the doctor had come by to be sure that I wasn't planning anything rash. I said, dejectedly, "No way, Doc. I can get around a bit on these crutches, but there's no way I could make the trip . . ."

Just then, I heard something outside the door. I could hardly believe my ears! It was the sound of sleighbells — and prancing reindeer hoofs!

Doc opened the door — and there was my
sleigh — all loaded with toys and ready to go! . . .
The Child waved from the driver's seat — and
the elves were shouting from the back,

"Come on, Santa! . . .
We can make the trip now!
. . . The 'secret project' is a special place for you to

ide! . . ."

There, attached to my sleigh,
was a most remarkable conveyance
— like a chaise lounge — on which
I could lie back with my leg all propped up in
comfort and safety. Doc checked it out and said,

"It looks great! . . . I'm sure it'll work fine . . ."
So, they bundled me
up and we took off
on the big trip . . .

As we reached each roof-top the elves did all the chimney climbing, while I was in back checking off the list. When we got to the last stop I was overjoyed! . . .

. . . I didn't think we
were even going to make
the trip — and here we were finished . . .

The Child came back and said, "Santa, I know you must be tired — but can we make one more stop?"

I said, "Listen, we'll go anywhere you want to go . . . If it hadn't been for you we could never have made the trip . . ."

The Child said, "I just want to show you where I was born . . ."

We took off into the silent night —
following a bright star that I had never
noticed before. Such a star! . . .
I had never seen such a star!

. . . Soon we landed by a humble stable . . .

The Child came back and said,
"Come with me, Santa. Please come with me."
He helped me up on my crutches, and
together we started hobbling toward the stable.

Suddenly, I looked around — and the Child had disappeared! . . . Then, I heard the Child's voice coming from the stable saying, "Don't be afraid, Santa. This is where I was born on the first Christmas night. Drop your crutches and come kneel with us."

Almost overcome by the sudden
realization of what I was viewing,
I let my crutches fall to the ground.
Hesitantly, I walked forward, took
off my hat and dropped to
my knees before an
incredibly beautiful scene —
the Nativity . . .

When I could finally catch
my voice, I asked, "Why —
why did you come
to me? . . ."

The Child's voice
replied, "To remind
you, dear Santa, to
remind you, and all the world, that Christmas is my

birthday . . . the birthday of the Lord . . ."

OTHER TREASURES FROM
SANTA AND THE CHRIST CHILD...

CASSETTE - SONG AND NARRATED STORY
CHRISTMAS CARD - FULL COLOR - 20 TO THE BOX